2007
COLLECTION

Short Sleeves

– A Book for Friends –

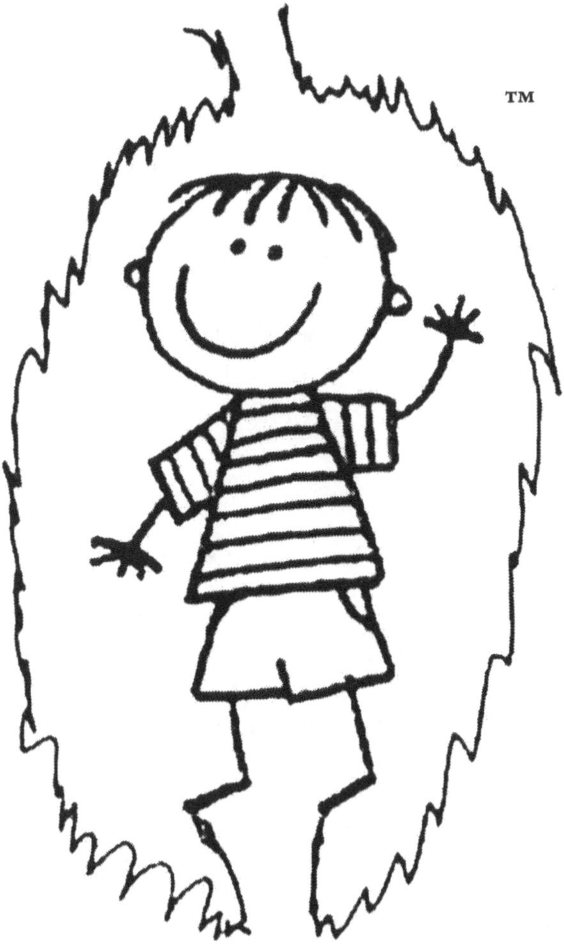

™

H. T. Manogue

©H.T.Manogue 2006 All Rights Reserved.
Short Sleeves A Book For Friends
2007 Collection
ISBN# 0-9778130-1-0
www.shortsleeves.net

To:

Joanie Hatch
The Perfect Dot Above The i In My Life.
My Eternal Gratitude And Love

My Special Thanks

Kathleen Jacoby

Devra Ann Jacobs

Chelle Thompson

Janet Boyer

Yvonne Perry

Charles "Tom" Brown

Tim Bellows

Janet Grace Riehl

Note From The Author:

2006 has been quite a year. I have experienced a new way of life. My world has changed or I should say evolved, with the release of Short Sleeves A Book For Friends 2006 Collection in May. It has been exciting to watch the reaction and hear the comments from so many friends. The work may not have touched a spark in everyone who read it or visited the web page, but they all remember it. That's why it was written, to remember. I want to thank everyone who took the time to read it and who sent me feedback.

The 2007 Collection, as you will see, has taken on a life of its own. Poems from the 2007 Collection have been published by Mystic Pop Magazine, Children Of The New Earth Magazine, Dream Weaver Magazine and several newsletters around the country.

This Collection was written in 2006 and really came from a place that radiates change. A change of thinking about who I am and how I see the world I live in. I was the physical instrument for the work, but the angels that surround me daily helped make this group so special. Through them I was able to move to a place that I call, "An abundant garden of thoughts". Fruitful words that were ready to be picked, tasted and savored in this place of bliss. My dream is to live in this garden, so that I am dancing with my spirit in gratitude.

2006 has certainly been a year of contrast for me and those around me, but the expansion we have experienced has been miraculous. This book is part of that expansion.

H.T.M.
Franklin, Tennessee
December 2006

A Poets Journey

Hello Everyone!
I send you love from Tennessee!
For those of you who know me
And for those who have yet to meet me,
I thought you might be interested in how I found my life's path.

For 25 years I thought the shoe business was it, but 10 years ago my thoughts started to change. I always was interested in people and had a strong desire to make money, because of my thoughts of lack.
The shoe business was the perfect vehicle to do both. Traveling nationwide and working in Asia, Europe and Brazil for years, taught me so many valuable life lessons.
I have been blessed with wonderful friends all over the globe. I have been able to create inerasable memories and lasting bonds. Thank you.

Yes, my life was externally comfortable but I still wondered what I was doing. I could not see the point of this me, by what I had been taught, experienced or remembered. The thought of how I appeared to others was more important than self worth.
I was plagued with the same situations we all face in one form or another; addiction to or from something, an inner fear of not being good enough and guilty for not understanding why. Of course the Death word was the ultimate fear for me and for everyone around me. I knew all of this was manifesting in various physical forms, weight gain or loss, injuries, health issues and off course not having enough of anything
Whatever the item desired.

In 1996 my mother died. My world changed.
She devoted her life to her family and her religion. Being raised in a devout Irish Catholic home she learned she could love and trust her God as long as she followed the teachings of the church. She believed. I struggled with rules and authority so her path and mine on religion were different. Mom loved her God and prayed that when she died, she would be reconnected with him as well as, all those who had gone before her. I had no idea what to say to God.
I now know her prayers were answered and more but at the time of her death, I felt alone for the first time in my life. It was all about me. She was gone. Who or what but Mother would do what she did for me?

Now feeling separated from her, I was looking for answers I wanted her back. I turned to philosophy beginning with Plato, Aristotle, Heraclitus, Plotinus, Lao-Tzu, Nagarjuna, Buddha, Confucius, Augustine. I started studying psychology and noticed anytime the author wanted to project a thought they would use poetry. I never had an interest in poetry, I didn't own a book of poetry.
One poet continued to be quoted in the books I studied. His name is Jalaluddin Rumi, better known as Rumi, who lived in Turkey in the mid-1200's. His family were scholars and theologians of their time. His words seem to call me, so I bought my first poetry book.
His writings completely took over my thoughts. While reading his work, I realized my life would never be the same again. It was in reading Rumi's words and his unending search for Shams of Tabriz, that I felt Mothers closeness and connection.

Then I Discovered Rilke, Blake, Goethe, Dante, Dickinson Takahashi, John Paul II and other Eastern and Western poets. In all of these friends, I found the same message regardless of the time portal: That love of self, reconnecting with your spirit, brings love to All. In order to love and to give the gift, I first had to be the vessel that held love for all things. With

love there is no death, only eternal life. Our loved ones live and always will.
Our inner voices connected in one. There is no separation after physical death.

This is the kind of message I've heard all my life, but it was Moms complete connection with God that opened a door for me thru poetry. I looked and all I needed to do was enter. I had to forgive myself so I could forgive others. I was looking to others for help, before I helped myself. The answers were within me.
I create the world I live in, either with spirit or without. Without is no longer an option.
Well-Being is our gift to ourselves thru our spirits.
I am never alone living in spirit. No one is.

You can contact me by email:
hal@shortsleeves.net
I would love to hear from you.

Hal Manogue

About Ace

Our Trademark
Ace represents the child we all know
The tremendous creator we have within us.
He signifies the high feelings of well being
We came equipped with when we started our path
In this physical world.
A for Awareness
C for Connected
E for Energy
My goal is to be like Ace with great worthiness
And love for all life.
To act as the child who knows no fear
Who knows no anger
Who knows no judgment.
Who fills days with works of joy and connection
For himself and for all he meets.
His level of experiencing joy and happiness in life
Changes with
Each thought of kindness
Each breathe of truth
Each act of freedom.

To be who he is
with
All That IS
For eternity.
His daily prayer is:
My Will Is To Will God's Will
In Every Cell Of My Body
To Be That I Which I Am
God's Evolving Plan

About Our Kids

The First one is Freedom
He's Free of all resistance
All guilt, suffering, anger, hatred and judgment.
He knows who he is and that all is well.
He is Free knowing there is no wrong path on his
physical journey.
By living in the NOW, he is connected to his spirit,
Spirit brings him joy and peace

The Second one is Awareness
She's
Aware of a greater plan a broader understanding
Of her spiritual world and her physical world
And how that union works within her.
Being aware she is never alone in spirit
She understands
That her emotions and feelings guide her,
when making choices in the physical world.
She knows she is loved
And she is love.

The Third one is Connection
Realizing he is connected
to his source, to his spirit and to all life.
He knows there is no death of consciousness.

Physical death is the doorway to

full connection with his spirit, completely wrapped
in joy and peace
He lives in happiness, knowing who he is Now
And who he will become, beyond the doorway.
Totally enjoying that grander version of himself.

The Fourth one is Contrast
Without experiencing herself in physical form
She would be unable to expand
her thoughts and desires.
She would be unable to grow
into the next grandest version of herself.
By using her emotions and feelings
to make choices she can complete her path
In the physical world.
With her name of contrast
Comes remembering.
In remembering
Comes love of self
And all life.

In Unity
They all work in the cycle of life
In Unity they all live in joy

NOW

Table Of Contents

A Brighter Version 1
A Tear From The Eye 2
Ace Thinks... 3
Age.. 5
Am I 6
An Endless Chip 7
As I Look Around 9
Beauty Floats Freely 10
Becoming 11
Between The Quiet 12
Bi-Cycle.. 13
Buddha 14
By The Pound 16
Eternal Grace... 18
Eternity 19
Flightless..20
Freely Free 21
God's My Name...22
Grey Tail 23
I Am 24
I Dance Everyday...25
I Frame Myself...26
I Live For You 27
I Missed School One Day 28
I Remember 29
I See You 32
I Smile 33
I Take In 34
I Toast Thee 35
I'm A Boomerang...36
I'm Flying With You..37
I'm Voting Today..38
In Sync 39
Invisible But Present 40
It's The Season 41

Joyfully	42
Just Feel Me	44
Life Moves In Circles	45
Looking Into The Mirror	46
Mention Thinking	47
My Center Is Erupting	48
My Ego Just Met My Heart	49
My Emotional Love	50
My Mind Paints	51
My Power	52
My Reflection	54
One Forever	55
Petal Power	56
Poetry Brings Us Together	58
Pure Love In Flight	59
Sanity	60
Searching	61
Seeds From The Sun	62
Shopping	63
Simple Thoughts	64
Simply Destiny	65
Simultaneously	67
Some How	69
Stillness Sings	70
Sunrise	71
Tennessee Ridge	72
That's Awareness	73
The Cosmic Urge	75
The Every Thing Of Nothing	76
The Face Of Life	78
The Face	79
The Garden Of Thanksgiving	80
The Island Of Love	81
The Path	83
The Raindrop	84
The Rock With Ears	85
Secret Melodies	87
The See	88

The Smell Of Autumn	90
The Solar Wind	92
The Sunset	93
The Universal Mystery	94
The Wind Grabs Me	95
To Be One	96
Walk In Beauty	98
Wandering Thru My Mind	99
Water Me	100
What Are We Doing Here	101
Wherever I Am	105
With Desire	106
With The Snap Of Fingers	107
Words Fly	108
Yes I Knew	109
You Are	110

The Friend Comes Into

My Body

Looking For The Center

Unable To Find It

Draws A Blade

Strikes Anywhere

Rumi

A Brighter Version

Storms In My Mind

Create A World Of Unrest

That Changes Me

Like A Tree

I Sway Bend And Crack

By The Weather Of Fearful Thinking

But Positive Thoughts Move Me

To The Beach Of Comfort Where

I Can Swim In The Calm Waters

Of Acceptance

I Choose To Release

The Energy Of Negativity

And Float In A Tide Of Belief

That With Every Mind Storm Comes

The Experience Of Being

A Brighter Version

Of Myself

A Tear From The Eye

Of Love

Turns A River Of Sorrow

Into An Ocean Of Joy

A Smile From The Face

Of Love

Moves Mountains Of Frowns

Into A Valley Of Peace

A Kiss From The Mouth

Of Love

Makes Angels Dance

With Delight

Love Makes Us Love

Ourselves

In The Mirror Of Life

Ace Thinks

God

Am I Ready For Birth

Can I Pick

A Special Body A Special Face

A Special Race

Can I Live

21st Century Time

Write A Book Learn To Cook

Ride A Bike Fly A Kite

Love To Light Humans Plight

With A Word Or A Herd

Of Angels Might

Can I Dance Create Romance

Have A Tail Ride A Whale

Be Tall Climb A Wall

Have A Ball Never Fall

Be 3 Know A Tree

Grow Some Hair Speak With Flair

Spread Some Love Everywhere

Can I Be All In One

With The Torch From Your Porch

Can I Be Just Like Thee

Yes You Can Son

Man

My God Is Fun

Creation Is Never Done

God And Me

Eternally

Age

In The World Of Oneness

Age Rests

In The Arms Of Abundance

Age Smiles

In A House Of Joy

Age Is Spiritual

In Love

Age Is Eternal

Am I

A Bird Of Paradise

Standing

In The Hand Of Oneness

Asks

Am I This Hand

Or

Am I The Fingers

Or

Am I The Lines

Or

Am I The Bird

That Stands

Within The Hand

Or

Am I

To: Oneness

An Endless Chip

Expression Is The Desire Of All Life

In Self Expression I Express Myself

So That I Can Remember My Spirit

Thru My Physical Experience

I Expand And Become

A Greater Version Of Myself

In An Endless Life Cycle

With No Beginning No End

I Look Around My World Of Beauty

I See

The Ant The Bee And The Butterfly

Living In Their Worlds Of Now

The Tree The Rock The Flower

Living In Their Worlds Of Now

I See All The Worlds Of Every Living Thing

That Surround Me

Living In The Now

I Want To Experience What I See

So Here I Am

Expressing What I See

In My World Of Now

I Become What I See

An Endless Chip Of Eternity

At Peace With All

That's Me

As I Look Around

As I Look Around

I See Nature Resting In Perfect Colors

My Eyes

Bring This Beauty To My Mind

Thoughts Explode Within Me

Thoughts Of Perfection Thoughts Of Creation

The Now Of Wonder Is Within Me

Created By Perfect All Life Is Perfect

Waiting To Express Itself In Diversity

Perfect Diversity Perfect Holons

I Am Life I Evolve Perfectly

Why Do I Change Perfection

It Is Only Me That Thinks I Am Outside Of Perfect

Separate From Perfect

But

Perfect Ness Creates My Life Perfectly

On The Canvas Of Eternity

Beauty Floats Freely

Beauty Floats Freely

It's Not Defined By Age Color Shape Or Size

It's An Invisible Essence That Touches

Every Ripple Of Eternity

Words Get Lost In Images Of Beauty

Only When The Spirit Meets And

Draws This Essence Into Being

Does A Union An Imprint Of Awe Take Place

That Wants To Be Articulated

In A True Communion Of Heart And Intellect

Feeling Beauty Surround Me

My Emotions Reach Out

To Be One With Man One With Nature

One With Myself

Becoming

Belief Is A Branch

From The Tree Of Life

It's Roots Filled With The Water

Of Hope

Blossoms Of Experience And Expression

Open With Vivid Colors Of Freedom

A Sign Of The Acute Beauty Within The Tree

Life Feeds On The Blossoms

Providing Nourishment For Its Journey

To Awareness

The Seeds Of Connection Are Carried

And Planted So That All

May Taste The Nectar

Of Becoming

The Flower Of Unity

That Provides Joy And Happiness

To The Tree To The Root

And To

Who We Are

Between The Quiet

Between The Quiet There's Noise

A Chain Of Events A Series Of Illusions

That Cover My Thoughts

A Veil Of Words Symbols And Actions

That Define Me

Who Shall I Be Between The Quiet

Between That Place Where

There Are No Events Or Illusions

Only A Pure Silence Of Being

A Pure Joy Of Giving

Who Shall I Be Between The Quiet

I Want To Be You

A Wormhole Of Life

Living In Your Sequential Noise

Of Reality

Bi-Cycle

In The Bed Of Time

My Life Awakens Itself

With The Light Of Spirit

Moving In A Cycle Of Oneness

It Reconnects Me To Love

In A Joyous Remembrance

Of All Things

I'm Riding The Bi-Cycle

Of God

Buddha

Buddha

There You Stand

Sending Emails

On Your Energy Trail

Our Guiding Light

Your Monk Day Bright

With A Heart Of Joy

And A Soul Of Toys

You're An Abundance Spreader

An Awareness Blender

An Absorbing Sponge

That's Always Wet

A Spoon Of Suffer Less Dust

The Knife That Humanity Trusts

A Fork Of Peaceful Thoughts

In Arms Of Forgiveness

That Hold The Taste

For Our Race

In Comforts Well

Your State Of Grace

Sets The Pace

In Our Face

To: Bhante Wimala

By The Pound

Repelling Down The Rabbit Hole

Of Life

I Remember My Soul

So Sweet The Memory

So Deep The Hole

A Rope Of Oneness

Guides Me Down

Cycle By Cycle

A Multi Dimensional

Simultaneous Pattern

Of Infinite Richness

And Variety Has My Soul

In His Hole

Just Like Space Infinity Is There

For Me To Share

An Eternity Completely Present

At Every Point In My Time

Everything's Now

I'm Not In Line

I'm Son Of The Moment

Up And Down Side To Side

Life Is Round

So Is The Hole

Where I'm Found Covered In Love
By The Pound

Eternal Grace

I Appreciate Free Will

I Appreciate Free Choice

I Appreciate Unity Within Myself

So That I May Give So That I Can Share

The Gift Of Love

The Me With Hair

Now

Will Be My Thankful Face

Forever More

In Eternal Grace

My Kiss Of Unity

For Our Human Race

Eternity

Rocks Of Magnificence Oceans Of Desire

To Be One As You Have Done

Holding Life Forms So Lovingly

Each Life Is So Diverse In Each Of Their Creations

They Live In Harmony

In A Order That Supplies Freedom And Unity

To Their Vision Of Longevity

Without A Word Without A Hand

Each Moment Is Part Of Life

Living The Holonistic Plan

Every Whole Is Part Of You

And You Are Part Of Another Whole Too

If Only I Could Think Like Thee

My Wholeness I Could See

As Just A Part

Of The Whole

I Call Eternity

Flightless

Flightless Antarctica Wonders
Walking Endlessly
Dressed In Suits Of Black And White
A Touch Of Orange To Show Your Class
And That Non Stop Fervor In Your Task
Without A Tree Without A Cave
You Stand In Unity In Weather's Way
In Loving Pairs With Frozen Hair
You Bend And Look At Your Feet
The Very Purpose Your Heart Beats
The Gift Of Now The Egg of Life
Gently Tucked Beneath Your Plight
As A Team You Love Supreme
Your Only Prayer Your Only Care
Is That Your Chick Will Do Your Trick
The Penguin Walk And Lots Of Talk
From Icy Wet To Icy Rock
You Are My Hero You Are My Flock
Of Frozen Angels
With Built In Eternal Clocks

Freely Free

What Happened When I Looked Away
Did I Fall Into A Pit Of Pity
A Hole Of Helplessness
Covered In Fear Anger And Hatred
My Blindness Fixed On Someone Else
Who Dwells In This Void That's Me
Desperately Wanting To Be Free
From A Self Inflicted
Sense Of Instability
I Close My Eyes I Look Inside
There I Find Nothing's Blind
In Glorious Sight I Have Angel
Might
Waiting There With A Prayer
Thoughts Of Hope Belief Elopes
I Climb The Slope
Third Eye Air Everywhere
A Forgiveness Breeze
Swirls In Me
Freely Free

God's My Name

God Is All Things

A Changing Dance Partner

Moving As I Step To His Music

Rhythm In Sync

Vibration To Vibration

Cycle By Cycle

Every Beat Is Now

Without Limitations Internally Or Externally

Bondage Free A Dancing Tree Of Life

Branches Sway Leaves Me Gay

Roots Do Pray

With No Ears I Do Hear

Far From Sight Eyes Shine Bright

Angels Mixing Sounds Tonight

Voice Of Light

God Is Bare I Have Hair

All The Same

God's My Name

Grey Tail

My Life As A Natural Gymnast

Takes Guts

And Is Filled With A Lot Of Nuts

Said A Squirrel

More Than That Trees Catch Mist

Branches Flex And Twist

Leaves May Split Birds May Spit

But Acrobatics Is My Game

And

Grey Tail Is My Name

I Am

I Am Brown I Am Green

I Am Tall I Am A Wall

I Am Bark I Am An Ark

I Am Roots I Am Leaves

I Am A Fort I Am Floor

I Am The Opening For A Door

I Am You I Am Me

Connected Branches

Of

A Tree

I Dance Everyday

I Dance Everyday

With Spirit

Solo We Waltz

To The Music Of Love

And Then We Twist

With God

On The Dance Floor

Of Eternity

I Frame Myself

My Mind Frames My World

With Beliefs With Experiences With Expression

Each Thought A New Color In My Ageless Rainbow

My Body Moves To The Beat Of Time

Reflecting The Portrait Of My Creation

Each Line Mark And Crack Is A Stamp

Of Remembering

Each Yesterday and Tomorrow

Is Vividly Painted Now

All There For Me To Accept

Or Change In Hue Or Tint

I Frame Myself

With The Palate Of Love

Then My Picture Of Life

Becomes

A Birth Of Freedom

I Live For You

In The Distance I See You

Sitting Within Me

Dripping With Love

Standing On The Edge

I Hear Your Voice

A Drop Of Your Love

Fills My Ocean Of Being

I Live For You

I Am A Ripple Of Water In Your Sea

I Am A Feather On Your Wing

I Am The Mist Above Your Cloud

I Am A Grain Of Sand On Your Beach

I Am A Rock That Sits On Your Mountain

I Am The Breeze Whispering Your Name

I Am The Bridge To Your Oneness

I Am The Mirror Which You Hold

So That I Can Be Your Reflection

In Magnificent Crystals

Of Love

I Missed School One Day

I Missed School One Day
That Day
I Taught The World To Pray
About Forgiveness
The Jesus Way
Cleansing Veins In Hateful Hearts
Draining Anger Arteries
That Keep The World On A Killing Course
That Drives Us From Our Loving Source
I Had To Die To Show That I
Will Come Again
Again And Again
To Show That Love Has No Death
When We Remember
The Forgiveness Tool Is That Which Rules
The School Bells Chime To Love Mankind
In All Names We Are The Same
Not Children Who Just Blame
And Lay In The Forgetful
State Of Judgmental Minds

In Remembrance Of: The Amish Children

I Remember

When I look At War

I See Loneliness

When I See Anger

I See Loneliness

When I See Hatred

I See Loneliness

When I See Judgment

I See Loneliness

Loneliness Is The Biggest Affliction

In My World Today

Emotional Physical And Spiritual Loneliness

The Feeling Of Being

Isolated Injured Or Burdened

In A Way No One Understands

A Sense Of Being

Without Resources Creates Pain

Suffering And Despair

A Formula Of Hopelessness

Nothing Matters But Escape

Escape From Loneliness

Escape Thru Judging

Everyone Else

And My Remedy Is Repetition

It Seems I Repeat

What I Seek To Avoid

Loneliness Is

Happening Through Me

Everything Happening Through Me

Is Happening For Me
For Me To Remember

Changing My Thoughts

Eliminates Loneliness

Nothing Happens Against My Will

Rather Than Creating Thoughts

From A State Of Mind

I Am Creating Feelings

From A State Of Spirit

In Spirit Loneliness

Does Not Exist

I Are Not Divided

In Spirit

I Am Connected

In Spirit

But I Still See Diversity

From Diversity

Comes Knowledge

From Knowing

Comes Experience

From Knowing And Experience

Comes Feeling

Which Is

The Language Of Spirit

And The Awareness That I Am

Never Lonely Only Forgetful

But Now I Remember

I See You

I See You

Swirling Thru The Leaves

Devour Me

As You Do The Leaves

So I Can Be

The Sound Of Nature's Energy

The Touch Of Nature's Unity

The Sight Of Nature's Face

Dancing In Your Embrace

With No Trace

Of Distaste

The Product Of

Your Divine Grace

I Smile

Fingers Of Forgiveness

Are Tickling Me

The Fingers Of Truth

Grab Me And Shake Me

From Thoughts Of Fear

Thoughts Of Suffering

My Eternal Will Is Free

To Love To Laugh

To Play

In True Belief

In The Hand

Of Natures Oneness

I Sit On A Beam

A Wave Of Eternity

Is

Dancing Within Me

I Smile

I Take In

I Take In What I Give Out

What I Absorb I Must Emit So That I Am In Balance

The Universe Is In Balance

I Am A Whole Part Of That Whole Part

That Is Unity

I Move In Circles Bending Back On Myself

I Live Because Goodness Lives In Me

I Give Goodness From My Spirit

The More Good I Give The More I Receive

The Cycle Of My Life Is A Circle Of Good

My Freedom Exists In Giving

The Circle Expands In The Freedom

Of Giving And Receiving Good

Which Is All There Is

I Toast Thee

Let Me Toast Self Expression

The Gift We Have To Share

Receiving Thoughts From Others

Enriches My Own Endeavor

To Live My Life For What It Is

A New Found Lesson

An Old Thought Remembered

In a Cycle Of Giving And Receiving

So That I May Be In My Expression

The Gift I Want To Receive

The Gift That's Always There

With Self Esteem I Toast Thee

My Giving Is My Sight

My Receiving Is My Might

I'm A Boomerang

I'm A Boomerang

Throwing Myself Out Into Physical World

Whirling Through Time and Space

I'm Touching All Energy In A Special Way

Feeling Joyful Peaceful And Grateful

I Sprinkle Those Positive Feelings

On They Who Watch My Flight

Spreading The Desire To Feel Those Same Thoughts

To Fly The Same Way

That Desire Lifts Me Higher

Twirling In The Minds Of Others Brings Me

Faith Hope And The Will To Return

To My Starting Point

The State Of Being Where I Am

Resting In The Arms Of Love

I'm Flying With You

I'm Flying With You

With A Breath Of Air I Feel The Warmth

Of Your Wings

Angels In Sight Feathers So Bright

I See You Watching Me From A Branch

Moving Your Eyes In Sync With Your Mating Blink

Your Chirping Glee Is Heavenly

Preparing Your Nest Your Harvest Is Best

Fall Brings You Feasts From Natures Beasts

Twigs And Brush Seeds From Us

Thankfully You Share Your World Of Air

With Those Who Know For Those Who Care

You Are Prayer In Loving Pairs

Creating Life To Show The Trust

You Have In Universal Dust

I'm Voting Today

I'm Voting Today

I'm Voting For Self Expression My Self Expression

I'm Casting My Vote For Inner Truth

My Inner Truth

The Wholeness Of Truth I Know Intuitively

It Is Not Partial Truth Not Fabricated Truth

Not Someone Else's Truth Of Conformity

To Attain An Illusion Of Power Over Me

It Is In Itself Universal Power

It Is Not Born Nor Does It Die

It Is Fully Connected To The Essence

Of Life All Life

It Follows No Laws Of Judgment

It Takes Nothing By Force

It Holds Nothing In Anger

It Embraces All

That Is Peaceful Joyful And Abundant

In The Arms

Of My Self Expression

In Sync

Frozen Image Of Spirit

Thawing In Joy And Love

Fill My Well Of Life

With Gratitude

For All To Drink

So All Will Think

In Kindness

In Peace

In Sync

Invisible But Present

My Mind Thinks

Filled With The Energy Of Consciousness

My Heart Beats

Filled With The Energy Of Love

My Lungs Breath

Filled The Energy Of Life

My Body Moves

Filled With The Energy Of Motion

I Am Surrounded And Connected To The Energy

Of Oneness

I Am Totally Complete In Mind And Body

Invisible But Present

Energy Guides Me In Truth

Relentless In The Desire For My Freedom

It Contains The Essence Of Me

And Releases Me To Express Myself

In Joy

It's The Season

It's The Season Angel Season

I Feel Them Everywhere

Oh Ageless Hair Wings Of Prayer

My Quiet Mind With Thoughts Sublime

Intuition Is My Fare

In Fearless Pride With My Guides

My Source Is Standing Bare

Angel Season Loving Greetings

One Gift Of Life To Share

Joyfully

My Mind Works Fine

I've Jumped Off The Cliff Of Insanity

And I Think I'm Growing Wings

Made Of Trust A New Energy Thrust

Every Thought's A Plus

My Spirit's At Work Emotions Perk

To The Beat Of Life

Awareness Heats A New Found Seat

Of Unending Bounds

Moving Clouds Finding Time

As I Pass Thru My Eternal Mind

A Fearless Sleep With Ageless Sheep

So

With Wings Sublime

I Am Blind To Illusions Rules

Judgment Schools Guilty Fuels

And

Angry Tools

Soaring Past Thoughts Of Death

I Am One My God Is One

Together We Are Free

Joyfully

Just Feel Me

I Am The Silent Wind Just Feel Me

In Any Form I Speak

Thru The Rock I Speak Firmly Of Truth

Thru The Sea I Speak With Endless Beauty

Thru The Sky I Speak In Perfect Oneness

Thru The Tree I Speak With Roots Of Life

Thru Nature I Speak In The Now

Thru Man I Speak In Self Expression

Thru Life I Speak In Eternity

Thru Creation I Speak Simultaneously

Thru The Universe I Speak In Profound Mystery

Thru Me I Speak To You

Life Moves In Circles

Life Moves In Circles

I Believe It Moves In Good Circles

In Goodness My Circle Glows

My Thoughts Create A Life Of Feeling Good

My Focus Is That Feeling

In My Words In My Work In My Movements

I Am Enveloped In Good Surrounded By Good

Nothing In Me Rejects That Good

I Totally Feel Its Presence

I Entertain It And Experience It

Fear Doubt Uncertainty Vanished From My Thoughts

Pleasure And Joy Are My Expectations

Within Me Within My Circle

Is This Place Of Happiness It Belongs To Me

Nothing In Me Denies It Nothing In Me Limits It

It Is My Power Of Will To Do And To Be Good

And Share It

Looking Into The Mirror

Looking Into The Mirror

Of Life

I See You

Looking Back

At Me

Smiling In The Glow

Of Us

In Peaceful Trust

Mention Thinking

Mention Thinking

And Everything Is

Found In Something

Add More Thinking

And Now Something

Is Found In Everything

Then Something

Awoke Thinking

About Everything

And Then Everything

Became Something

Without Something

Ever Knowing

Everything

Is

Something

My Center Is Erupting

My Center Is Erupting

In A Flowing Lava Of Consciousness

That Is Covering My Mind

With A Warm Essence Of Being

Swimming In This Flow

I Am An Ocean Of Self Love

I Open Myself To You

My Thoughts Are Your Thoughts

My Body Is One With You

My World Is A Sea Of Forgiveness

My Universe Is A World Of Spiraling Love

That Holds Itself Together With Your Touch

Now I Am An Island

Surrounded By Myself

My Ego Just Met My Heart

My Ego Just Met My Heart

Heart Says

Time For Us To Change Our Parts

I Will Lead You Take Heed

Universal Plan Has Got Our

Vibration Moving Man

A Faster Speed A Worldly Need

You've Done Your Part

Now It's Heart To Heart

When It's Love To Love

I Hear No Thugs

Only Blessed Grace In Perfect Taste

Creative Time Miracle Mines

Just Let Go

And

Watch It Flow

My Emotional Love

In A Moments Embrace

I'm Aroused

By Gentle Moods

Caressing Hands

Tender Kisses

Sweet Low Whispers

Feeling The All That's Me

I Sense That All My Parts

Are In One Heart

Your Love For Me

Covers Me In Emotional Peace

Warms Me In Emotional Rays Of Light

Relaxes Me In Emotional Scents Of Freshness

Guides Me In Emotional Thoughts Of Beauty

Becomes Me In Emotional Ecstasy

My Mind Paints

My Mind Paints This Page
With The Brush Of Creativity
Colors Of Life Appear In Words
Phrases Sentences
A New World Is On The Page Before Me
It Is
Reaching Out Touching Those
Who I Have Touched Before
But Do Not Remember
Thoughts Of Connection Fill My Memory
An Awareness Of Sharing Moves My Pen
Scribing Simple Thoughts Of Giving
That Which I Have To Give
A Knowing That We Are All One
In My Rainbow Pen Of Love

My Power

Opening My Eyes I See

What I Want To See

My Ears Hear

What They Want To Hear

My Mouth Says

What I Think It Should Say

My Heart Feels Emotions

It Wants To Feel

My World

Is What I Make It

My Life Is My Choice

Knowing Who I Am

Makes My Choices Easier

Knowing I Am Connected

To Goodness Abundance And Love

From One Source

Is

My Power Of Resolve

To Embrace That Connection

When I Open

My Eyes My Ears My Mouth

And My Heart

In The Face Of Contrast

My Reflection

My Mirror That Sits Within

Makes Me Grin

I Must Confess It's Full Of Dreams

And Joy Full Schemes

Of Giving Love To My Guest

It Has No Name And No Shame

It's

My Eternal Game My Eternal Flame

It's Always Present It Always Shows

What I Look Like When I Glow

Mirror Of Might My Core's So Bright

You And Me Are Heavenly

God's My Light

My Reflection Is My Kite

To Fly For All In Sight

My Angels Dance

In Our Delight

One Forever

Every Thing Sits Here

With Me

In

This Now

My Past Long And Last

Are Here As Memories

Now

My Future Dreams Plans And Schemes

Are My Expectations

That's What I Call

Them

Now

They Are Here

In A Perfectly Formed Cycle Of Life

Yesterdays And Tomorrows

Are Born

Into

One Forever

Now

Petal Power

Two Petals

From The Same Flower

Each Part Of One Stem

Each A Stroke Of Genius On It's Own

Each Different In Design

Each Blossom

Awakens In A Different Time

A Cycle Of Sublime Love

Each In Love With Itself

In A Delicate Life Of Joy

Hanging In Beauty's Laird

Filled With Flair

Ever So Special In Pairs

Sitting On Heaven's Stairs

Willing Loving Stares

And Sunlight's Prayers

Each One Snug With The Rug

Of Natures Mind

The Only Course In God Lee Source

So I Pray With Words Today

Enfold Petal Power In My Time

Let Me Touch

My Source Of Mind

Memory Please Find

That I Am The Vine

With Pure Love Running Through

My Stem Of Mankind

A Grape To Taste A Nectar Of Grace

A Wine Refined From The Root

Of A Peaceful Mind

Poetry Brings Us Together

We All Experience Life Through Knowledge

In The World Of Body And Mind

We Express Our Lives Through Words And Symbols

And Then We Become That Which We Express

We Also Experience Life

Through Our Intuitive Knowledge

In The World Of Spirit That Lives Within Us

We Express Ourselves

Through True Feelings And Emotions

We Then Become That Which We Really Are

Poetry Brings Both Of Those Ways Of Knowing

Together

So That We Are One Again In

Body Mind And Spirit

Pure Love In Flight

My Life Is Multi Dimensional

With Wings Of Peace

With A Heart Of Abundance

With A Body Of Gratitude

With My Spirit Of Light

I Move Thru Time

Sequentially

And Simultaneously

Pure Love In Flight

Sanity

Sanity Is Waiting

For Me To Return To The World

Within Me

Waiting For Me To See Myself

As I Am

Free From The Illusion

Free From The Dreams

Of Others

Free In The Arms

Of Sanity's

Oneness

Searching

While Searching For Success
Failure Grabs Me By The Hand
Each Finger Is Pointing To My Defeat
My Palm Is Sweating Pushing Me To Quit
My Other Hand Waving
In The Air Of Panic
In A Moment Of Courage I Release Myself
Dangling Off The Cliff Of Fear
The Hands Of Will Power Touch Me
Then Embrace Me
Guiding Me To My Internal Ladder Of Truth
I Climb From My Thoughts Of Despair
To The Garden Of Success
Where I Find Myself Looking
Into A Mirror Of Illusion

Seeds From The Sun

Seeds From The Sun

Flower Into A Beautiful Garden

A Living Breathing Floating

World Of Wonder

Each Connected By Invisible Life

That Roots Itself In Joy

Each Flower Each Stem Each Root

Independent From But Dependant

On It's Source Of Faith

To Shine With The Light Of Oneness

To Be Watered From The Bucket Of Love

To Be An Everlasting Gift

Of Perfection

Shopping

Shopping Thru The Store Of Life

I Found You

My Gift To Myself

The Ultimate Present Wrapped

In The Warmth Of The Sun

Lit By The Glow Of The Stars

A Gold Ribbon

Twirled Around The Moon

Of My Thoughts

Waiting Patiently To Be Opened

Resting Quietly On The Shelf

Of My Mortality

My Mind Peeks I Feel Your Glance

As The Veil Of Forgetfulness Drops

I Jump Into Your Joy

Kissing My Gift

Of Remembering

Simple Thoughts

I Watch Myself Chasing Simple Thoughts

Thru The Mind Field Of Doubt

Wondering If My Mental Prose

Would Be The Right Suppose

To Fill My Life With Sweet Repose

Grander Thoughts I Have Been Taught

Are Less Than I Proclaimed

My Simple Thoughts My Humble Mind

Makes My Life Gently Kind

With Doubtless Eyes I See Why

My Simple Thoughts Are An

Extraordinary Find

That I Choose To Share

With Mankind

Simply Destiny

Who Is This Me I Want To Be

So Many Words Can Define Me

I Know That

Freedom Feeds Me Abundance Dresses Me

Giving Energizes Me Receiving Excites Me

Forgiveness Empowers Me Understanding Enlightens Me

Compassion Comforts Me Truth Relaxes Me

Joy Connects Me Happiness Engulfs Me

I Also Know That

Fear Defeats Me Anger Entangles Me

Judgment Swallows Me Hate Controls Me

Deceit Enslaves Me Conceit Separates Me

Envy Weakens Me Self Hatred Attacks Me

Mistrust Abuses Me Killing Kills Me

I Have Many Thoughts That Become The Things

That I Can Be

I Have Many Choices Many Voices

That Speak To Those I Think I See

But There Is Only One Me Inside The Chatter

It's The Me I Said I Be Before I Became This Matter

I Am A Light That Shines With Mighty Energy

My Source Is Love I Must Be Love

Pure Love Is Me Powerfully

My Source And Me

Are Simply Destiny

Simultaneously

I Create God In My World

With Gentleness and Gratitude

With Loving Acts Of Kindness

With Warm Words Of Giving

With Forgiving Bands Of Friendship

With A Joyous Heart Of Oneness

With Abundant Rings Of Mercy

With Overflowing Respect For All Life

With Connected Awareness

Of Being

With Self Love Knowing That

I Am His Likeness

I Am His Vision

I Am His Actions

I Am His Thoughts

I Am His Spirit

I Am His Peace

I Am

So That I May Be Like Him

I Am

So All Can Be Like Her

I Create God

As He Created Me

Simultaneously

Some How

Some How My Now

Became

Time And Space

A Place

Filled With Humans Race

But What's The Race In Humans Pace

Is It Grace

Or Just A Place For Human Waste

Is It Kind To Be Blind

To Only See In Misery Thoughts of Humanity

Are Its Walls Filled With Hate

Bombs Answer They Say Fate

Is It Real Or Just A Peel

From The Skin

That Lies Within My Ego Twin

Is It Black Or Pure Fright

Living Without That Light Of Might

That Gave Me

Now

To Love

Some How

Stillness Sings

A

Mountain Of Grandeur

Resting

In The Presence Of Art

Is Within Me

It's Melting Ice Floods My Mind With Thoughts

Of An Ageless Time

The Silence Of Nothing

Is

Frozen In The Footprints

Of My Consciousness

A Blue Horizon Awakens Me

With A Unity Of Vision

I'm Racing Towards The Bridge

Of Oneness

Where

Stillness Sings

Sunrise

Daylight Is Every Thing

To A Sunrise

There Is No End To Daylights Love

No End To The Love

That Awakens A World Each Day

The Presence Of A Sunrise

Is A Present From Love

To Be Shared With Love

To Be Enjoyed In Love

To Be Love

Especially At Sunrise

Tennessee Ridge

My Tennessee Ridge Taught Me Something

Rock of Thee

Which You Should I Be

Brave And Tall Standing Falls

Or Broken Ones That's Some Fun

A Zillion Shapes Just Like Us Apes

I Could Be Flat And Sit On Top

With Color Streaks And Seats For Beaks

A Nesting Rock I Watch The Flock

With No Clock Just A Crack

Of Instant Fame I Need No Name

Just Play Your Game

Of Being Now Silent Proud

Here I Am

Ridge Top Man Feeling Grand

That's Awareness

My Mind

Is Like A Parachute

It Only Works When It's Open

It Only Takes A Decision To Change My Mind

To Look At Myself As Who I Am

On The Path Of Involution Not Retribution

The Things I Think The Things I Say

The Things I Do

Send Out A Vibration From

The Core Of My Being

Creating From What Is Instead Of From A State

Of A Closed Mind

My Feelings

Are The Language Of My Spirit

Gratitude

Is

My First State Of Being

Everything I Experience Physically I Know Inwardly

That's Awareness

The Feeling Of What I Have Known

And Experienced

It Is One Thing To Know Something

It's Another Thing To Experience It

And Another To Feel It

Feeling

Produces Awareness

Now I Know Time Is Not Something That Passes

It Is Something That I Pass Through

In My Cycle Of Life

So

I Can Know Myself

In

My Own Experience

This Is The Reason For My Life

And

All Life

The Cosmic Urge

The Cosmic Urge Is Within Me
Always Yearning To Create My Life
To Be Self Fulfilled Through Love And Accomplishment
It's The Fundamental Urge We All Have
Whether It's Man Animal Or Nature
To Lavish Our Affections
On Something Or Someone
And Then Find Fulfillment
From The Object Of Our Desire
This Emotional Craving For Self Expression
This Impulsion Is Innately Born With Life Itself
Hence We Are Surrounded
By Love And Attention Immediately At Birth
In This Way
The Cosmic Urge The Urge Of Our Spirit
Is Able To Grow Healthily In The Physical World
In Partnership With Truth With Beauty
And With Self Empowerment
So
I Can Continue To Create Myself
In The Cycle Of Life

The Every Thing Of Nothing

War Is Insistence On Conformity

It Is Determination To Promote Sameness

We All Are One But Not The Same

Each Passing Thru Our Own Time Frame

Each Being

Is Connected To All Life

Death Is Creation Birth Is Creation

Each War

For The Sake Of Conformity

Brings Us To The Understanding

That War

Creates More War And Less Conformity

War Is Separation From Who We Are

A Disconnection Of Spirit And Love

Thru The Suffering Of Wars

A Remembering Takes Place

For All To Experience

The Path To Peace Begins With Me

The Me I Want To Be

To Be At Peace I Need Oneness

Of Spirit Mind and Body

Then All Is Being With All Beings

In Understanding And Compassion

Connecting

To Who I Am I Move My Consciousness Up

The Spiral Of Existence

To The Shelf Of Inner Knowledge

That Only Knows Love

That Is All There Is

Togetherness In Freedom

Freedom

In Diversity Of Life

Without Form Without Judgment Without Blame

All I Need Is

The Every Thing Of Nothing

I Call God

The Face Of Life

The Face Of Life

Is Carved By The Energy Of Thought

With Eyes Of Love

I See All Things As One Yet Diverse

A Smile Of Truth

Opens My World To Freedom

A Heart Of Giving

Surrounds Me With Abundance

A Mouth Of Peace

Engulfs Me In Beauty

With Ears That Listen

My Inner Voice Guides Me

To A Body

Of Forgiveness

The Face

The Face Of Life Stares At Me

With Eyes Of Remembrance

With A Mouth That Smiles With Love

With Ears That Hear The Silence Of Peace

With A Thought Of No Thought

With A Taste Of Eternity

That Gently Swallows Me

The Garden Of Thanksgiving

The Beacon Of Peace Shines Brightly

When I See It Within Me

The Basket Of Abundance Overflows

When I Am The Basket

The Voice Of Freedom Sings With Soul

When I Hear My Heart's Vibrating Strings

The Garden Of Thanksgiving Blooms With Beauty

When I Water It With Grateful Thoughts

Thoughts Are The Seeds Of Change

That Become Roots Of My Life

As With Nature They Are Not Visible At Birth

But Grow Into The Form I See

What Shall I Be

Thankfully It's Up To Me

The Island Of Love

The Island Of Love

Is Surrounded By A Sandbar

Filled With Life

Each Life Looking For The Food

Of Well Being

At Times The Current Around The Island

Seems To Move The Sandbar

But Life Is Still Present

Perhaps The Sandbar

Appears Deeper Or Longer Or Shorter

Yet Life Is Still Present

Then New Life Appears

New Forms Evolving

To Expand The Search For Well Being

All Life

On Their Own Seek The Same Thing

Around The Same Island

And Collectively Find What They Need

Each Life Compliments The Other

Knowing The Island Provides For All

Abundantly

Life Is The Sea Of Self Expression

Salted With The Taste Of The Divine Energy

Endless In The Quest

To Stay Connected To The Island

That Is Itself

The Path

The Path

To No Where

Moves Consciousness

Into Nothing

But

Itself

Connecting To The Truth

Which Is Who I Am

The Raindrop

The Raindrop Always Finds A Stream

The Stream Always Follows A Path To A River

The River Always Finds Its Way To An Ocean

The Ocean Always Finds Itself On A Beach

The Beach Looks Up And Finds A Cloud

The Cloud Is Filled With Raindrops

Waiting To Find The Stream

So Creation Is A Stream That Fills A River

That Becomes An Ocean

Touching Beaches Of Oneness

That Kiss The Clouds Of Darkness

Bringing Life Back To Its Source

A Cycle Repeated In Love

The Rock With Ears

I Will Wipe Away That Inner Fear

Rocks Have No Fear They Just Appear

Firm And Strong Holding Nests

Homes For Guests

Call Them Names They Change

In Range

Their World Is Wet Then Dry

They Paint Themselves To Flirt With The Sky

Or Turn To Sand For Beaches Grand

They Can Be A Wall Lots Of Feet Tall

They Break In Pieces

And Then Reveal Crystal Fields

With Shapes Unreal

The Rock Does Build A Throne

A Pyramid Dome

Any Place Yes Even In Space

Where They Were Born

With Instant Memory Form

Add Gas And Ice

They Fly Really Nice

With Rocks Of Salt I Can Dine

In Endless Time

The Sea Of Rocks Is Mighty Shepherd

For All Flocks

Inner Fear Step To The Rear

Here I Am

The Rock With Ears

Secret Melodies

The Secret Melodies

Found In My Heart

Are Filled With The Music

Of Love

Rhythms Of Laughter

Notes Of Pleasure

Bars Of Simplicity

Surround Me Cover Me

In Dancing Flowers

The Scent Of Fresh Life

Pulls Me Into The Beat

Of Oneness

Into The Nothing

That Is The Every Thing

Of You

The See

Riding On A Breeze

Fall

Stops And Sits On A Branch

It's Not By Chance

Summer's Moving In A Cycle

The Southern Spheres Time Is Here

Winters

Packing For Another Trip

It's A Short Stop

To A Mountains Top

Spring

Relaxes With A Sip

Before It Takes A Dip

In The Ocean Of My Mind

Every Where I Look

Weather Writes A Book

On How To Love Mankind

Called By Any Name It's All The Same

Call It One Call It None

Weather's There

To Change Some Hair

More Than That

It Packs Some Facts

That I Should Know As I Grow

Into Fall Into All

For Now I'm One I'm Never Done

Weather's Fun

It's My Compass And Tether

I'm Learning To Be A Feather

Every Breeze

Every Drop From Its Quill

Kisses Me

I'm Heading Towards

The See

And God's With Me

The Smell Of Autumn

The Smell Of Autumn

Changing Colors Of Life

Awaken The Sense Of Change

Within Myself

The Touch Of Cool Air

Sooths My Thoughts Of Sameness

That Have Covered My Physical Mind

Dancing Trees Undressing In The Wind

Magically

Make My Eyes Glow

In The Beauty Of Nakedness

The Squirrels Are Chasing Themselves

Gathering Nuts For Their Journey

They

Entice Me To Search The Earth

For Food For My Soul

There's Enough To Share

With The Sun The Moon The Stars

Who Kiss My Face

With

The Universal Energy Of Heaven

My Mind Body And Soul Are Together In Autumn

Never Leaving Me Lonely

Never Leaving Me Separated

From The Self

I Call

My Now

The Solar Wind

The Solar Wind's Caught In A Magnetic Grin

It Lights Our Mind

With Strings Of Color A Forceful Glow

Above The Snow

Green And Blue Thoughts Of You

Twist And Shake

A Creation Direct From Outer Space

A Flowing Snake

That Hides Within The land Of Sins

In Thoughtless Winds

Waiting For The Time To Shine

Energy's Dressed

For Its Guests A Oneness Vest

In Oneness Best

Aurora Borealis Ness

The Sunset

The Sunset Over The African Plains

Brings A Rush Of Comfort

To Their Giant Form

Resting Peacefully With The Family

The Voice Of The Matriarch

Brings Unity To The Herd

Of Loving Elephants

Living For The Now

Accepting Their World Of Hardship

They Care For Each Other

Aware That Their Babies Are Gifts

They Play Feed and Teach Them To Be

As They Are

The Essence Of Life

Accepting All That's Given

And

Giving All They Have To Give

In The Cycle Of The Sunset

The Universal Mystery

The Universal Mystery

Swims Within Me

My River Of Life

Wants To Be Rediscovered

Wants To Be Limitless

Wants To Magnificently Carry Me On My Journey

Thru The Channel Of Freedom

My Vessel Is My Mind I Direct My Voyage

I Can Change Course Change Speed

And Stop If I Block The Flow

With False Convictions

My Sail Is Free Will

Tacking To The Island Of Awareness

That Connects Me

To The Sea Of Peace

I'm

Floating In Eternity

The Wind Grabs Me

The Wind Grabs Me

I Rest On A Breeze Of Peace

Moving

With Its Gentle Motion

I'm Dressed In My Suit Of Fall

I Fly Free

Unattached Fearless

Ready To Meet My Maker

And Return To The Oneness Of Me

My Stem Touches The Earth

Roots Of My Family

Call My Name

My Form Dissolves In Love

With Spring I Will Return To Kiss The Breeze

I'm Dressed In Green

Sitting Gloriously On My Tree Of Life

Always Thankful

For The Light

To Be One

How Did I Look How Did I Feel

When

I Was A Sperm Or An Egg

Did I Laugh And Giggle

Did I Rush To Hit The Mark

Or

Just Sit And Wiggle

Either Path Was A Bath

Mystery with Sprinkles

Just A Task That Holistic Path

My Spirits Tilled My Journey's Filled

With A Conscious Plan To Expand

From A Sperm To The Term

Caterpillars Know That Butterflies Glow

Tadpoles Know Frogs Can Grow

Water Grand Makes Greener Land

Maggots Thrive To Live As Flies

A Creation Mix A Box Of Tricks

Not To Own But To Share

In Beauty's Home

Oneness Never Changes

Life Is Cycle-tagious

And

Outrageously Fun

To Be

As One

Walk In Beauty

Yua-Tah-Hey

That's Navajo For

Walk In Beauty

It's Knowing That My Dreams And Goals

Are Already Accomplished

When I Work Toward Something

An Open Ended Journey

I Am Always On The Way Seeing Milestones

Trying To Get Closer To It

Pushing It

Struggling With It

But If I Think My Dream Has Already Come To Life

My Goal Already Achieved

My Power Of Belief Takes Over

I Feel The Joy Of The Accomplished Act

Rather Than The Trauma Of The Journey

My Everyday Life Is Changed From The

Possibility Of Imagination

To The Reality

Of My Consciousness

Wandering Thru My Mind

Wandering Thru My Mind

I Stop

And See Myself Eclipsed By A Shadow

Covering My Light Of Creativity

In The Stillness I Do Nothing But Watch

As This Moon Of Shadows

Surrounds My Light Switch Of Thought

In The Stillness I Do Nothing But Watch

As This Shadow Moves Itself

A Beam Of Light Sparkles In The Movement

A Ray Of Belief Shines Thru Me

My Pilot Light Of Knowing Is Ignited In The Glow

My Thoughts Grow Stronger Fueled By The Energy

Of The Bright Light Of Creativity

That Is Within Me

Experiencing The Darkness

I Become My Ray Of Belief I Become One

With Myself

Water Me

I'm Sparked

By The Essence Of Love

The Seed Within Me Grows

This Now

Is My Time

To Be Spring To Do My Thing

Nature Knows It Has Perfect Hands

It Never Fails On Land Or Oceans Grand

And Like The Trees

Every Twig And Leaf

Root And Bark Are Growing Beauty

Works Of Art

I Have That Seed That Life Is Me

MY Joy Full Abundant Journey

Is Fear Free Please Water Me

With Humble Gratitude

And Giving Acts Of

Tranquility

What Are We Doing Here

That Question Rings Out Like An Alarm Clock

From Hell

When We Look At Ourselves In The Middle East

Yes That's Us We See Daily

Being The Bombed And Bomber On The Nightly News In The Papers And In Our Hearts

It Is In Our Experience Our Now

Of Course The Faces Are Different And The Names

Don't Match Ours And Perhaps Their Religions Are Not Ours

But There We Are Killing Each Other And Complacently Watching

Us Destroy Ourselves

In The Name Of God Belief And Superiority

We Know It's True

What You Believe You Create Then Experience

And Then Become

Our Collective Belief For Centuries Has Been That There Could Not Be Peace In This Part Of Our World

That This Was Such A Sacred Area That It Must Not

Be Shared

It Became Our Battle Ground To Prove God's Point

And Now As We See This Destruction Of Life We Are Asking Ourselves What Was That Point

Was It That He Chooses To See Us Suffer In The Pain Of War

Is The Point To Begin To End Life As We Know It

Because We Fail To Love Him In A Certain Way

Or Call Him By Names Other Than His Favorite Name

The God That We Know But Have Forgotten

Does Not Believe Or Create In That Way

All We Have To Do Is Look And Feel And Touch What

Surrounds Us

To See That The Universe Nature And Humanity

Are Connected In A Web Of Love

Spun By The Vessel Of Love

It Seems We Want To Break That Web

We Want To Be The Black Widow Of Life

Resting In Our Own Pots Of Ego

Lost And Fearful

As I Watch Myself Killing Me

I Now See The Point

I Realize My Belief About Who I Am And What I Am

Is Creating This Experience And I Have Become

What I See

I See

Hatred Anger Judgment

And Most Of All Feel The Loneliness

That Sits In My Heart

A Loneliness To Reconnect With Myself

To Connect To That Web Of Love That Is Me

That Feeling Of Oneness With All Life

For When I Drop All The Symbolic Names I Call Others

I Realize That We Are All Life First

Spirits Traveling On The Path Of Discovery And Re-membering

Journeymen In Love

All From The Same Source All The Same Yet Diverse

Moving Through Time To Awaken And Reconnect To

Ourselves And Then To Share Our Connection In Gratitude

Now Is My Time To Change My Beliefs

I Believe We Can Share Every Inch of Earth in Harmony With All Life

I Respect The Beliefs Of Others

In Understanding The Contrasts Of Beliefs

I Expand And Experience A Greater Version Of Myself

In This Moment In Me I Believe I Can Be The Difference

That Changes My Creations

So That I Experience God As He Experiences Me

In Peace Joy Love And Abundance

In That Now Awareness I See

That There Is No Death No Killing

No Separation No Loneliness

Only The Birth Of Forgiveness

And Unity

The Unity

I Have Been Searching For Everywhere

Except In Myself

Wherever I Am

Wherever I Am

My Soul Knows Itself Completely

On It's Path In The World Of Spirit

And Completely Experiences

Itself On Its Path In The Physical World

When Both Paths Are Put Together

That Environment

Is Perfect For Me To Create

A Complete Feeling Of Myself

Which Produces Complete Awareness

Of Who I Am

Feeling Is The Language Of My Soul

Home Is That Feeling Of Completion

Knowing And Experiencing

Joined In The Core Of My Being

It's My Heaven

Wherever

I Am

With Desire

The Old Thought Of Dying

Has Died In Love

I Was Meaningless

Until

I Found The Stream Of Love Within Me

That Stream Flows Through The Banks

Of Change

Following The Path Of Oneness

Emptying In The Ocean

Of All That Is All That Was

All That Will Be

And

Repeating That Cycle

In A Tide Of Gratitude

My Life Is Wet

With Desire

With The Snap Of Fingers

With The Snap Of Fingers

I Wake Up

No Longer Hypnotized By Collective Beliefs

Beliefs That There Is Not Enough

Of Anything

These Beliefs Bind Me In Old Precedents

And Compel Me To Only Accept

What I Have Experienced In My Past

Simply By Changing My Thoughts

Opening My Imagination

And Accepting New Feelings

I Will Overcome The Old Limitations

By Identifying

With The Universal Concept OF Abundance

My Mind Is Buoyant

Expectant And Enthusiastic

Knowing That I Have The Secret Of Life

Within Me

Without Limitations

Words Fly

Words Fly From The Nest Of Thought
And Land In The World Of Things
Thoughts Are Things Translated By Words
Translation Is Motion Translation Is Sound
Translation Is Language
Words Are The Maps And Symbols
Of My World
But Not The World Itself
The Great Nest Of Thought My Roost Of Being
Is My World
How I Express Myself Physically
Thru My Translation Of Words
Is How I Read Myself
I Can Read Whatever I Want Me
To Be

Yes I Knew

Honeysuckle Spring
That Bah Bing Sweet Smelling
Good Time Thing
Color Coded Bugs Flapping Let's Party Wings
Touristy Lovers Those Flocking Birds
Set Their Nests
For New Born Guests
Abundance Roars
When It Rains It Pours
Dogwoods Light The Floors
In Godly Moors
Peachy Kind What A Find
Apple's Got Green In Mind
Branches Dancing Buds Are Blind
Wind Is Whispering Now Your Mine
Red Bud Kisses Magic Vines
Azalea Blooms With Red And White
Cardinal Chirps Love's My Flight
Ajuga Blue Springtime Flu
Yes I Knew
What I See Is Me
Finally Seeing You

You Are

The Whisper In My Wind

The Light In My Lightning

The Wetness In My Raindrops

The Buzz In My Bees

The Bang In My Big Bang

The Blue In My Sky

The Orange In My Sunset

The Eclipse Of My Moon

The Flower In My Garden

The Spring In My Step

The Fall In My Mind

The Summer Of My Love

The Winter Of My Life

The Creation Of My Dreams

The Dreams Of My Creation

You Are My Face In The Mirror

The Mirror Of My Face

And I Am

What You Are

Contact Us

For more information about Short Sleeves
or the Author
Visit:
www.shortsleeves.net

Or by snail mail:
Short Sleeves
1013 Chapel Ct.
Franklin Tn. 37069

About the Author

Howard (Hal) Thomas Manogue, was born in Philadelphia in 1947 and is a forerunner to the indigo children, a now age term for a misfit with an intuitive nature, a desire to know his truth and a gift of giving and sharing. Hal has been employed in the shoe industry for 35 years, and in 1982 brought the waffle cone to the USA from Denmark with his ice cream stores "Finnicky's" based In Nashville Tennessee.

He enjoys art, music, philosophy, psychology, nature and people.

Hal started writing poetry in 1996. His first book: Short Sleeves A Book For Friends, was self-published in 2003. His second book; Short Sleeves A Book For Friends 2006 Collection, was released in May 2006. His poems have been published by: Mystic Pop Magazine, Children Of The New Earth Magazine, Dream Weaver Magazine, Seasons Of The Soul Newsletters, Lightship News and Writers In The Sky Newsletters.

He lives in Franklin Tennessee with wife Joanie, son Elliot, and daughter Megan.

Visit: www.shortsleeves.net or email hal@shortsleeves.net

www.ingramcontent.com/pod-product-compliance
Lightning Source LLC
Chambersburg PA
CBHW030141170426
43199CB00008B/164